COLLINS AURA GARDEN HA

G000320314

ORNAMENTAL
GRASSES

ALAN TOOGOOD

HarperCollins*Publishers*

Products mentioned in this book

Benlate* + 'Activex' 2   contains   benomyl
'Weedol'   contains   diquat/paraquat

*Benlate is a registered trade mark of Du Pont's

Read the label before you buy; use pesticides safely

Editors Diana Brinton, Joey Chapter
Designer Joyce Mason
Picture research Moira McIlroy
Production Craig Chubb

First published in 1991 by
Harper Collins Publishers
London

**A CIP catalogue record for this book
is available from the British Library.**

ISBN 0-00-412603-3

Photoset by Litho Link Ltd, Welshpool, Powys, Wales
Printed and bound in Hong Kong by Dai Nippon Printing Company

Front cover: Arundinaria viridistriata, Cortaderia selloana and
Miscanthus sinensis by the Harry Smith Horticultural Collection
Back cover: Miscanthus sinensis 'Zebrinus' by Michael Warren

CONTENTS

INTRODUCTION

Handsome foliage, a long period of interest and distinctive flowers; these are the virtues of ornamental grasses. Being so different in habit from many other plants, grasses provide dramatic contrast in planting schemes, and today no garden is complete without them.

Grasses are members of the family Gramineae and they may be either herbaceous or evergreen perennials, or annuals. Many form clumps or tufts of growth; others have a carpeting habit. Some of the perennials spread by means of rhizomes (creeping underground stems).

The leaves are long and narrow, often lance-shaped, or rush-like if extremely narrow. The colour range includes all shades of green, bluish or greyish shades, and yellow, and many are striped or variegated.

Flower stems are rounded and non-woody. The flowers are tiny and insignificant, not highly coloured as in many plants, but collectively they produce a quite distinctive effect. Some grasses, such as *Cortaderia selloana*, the pampas grass, have feathery plumes; others, including some of the stipas, produce airy sprays; *Hordeum jubatum*, the foxtail barley, has feathery spikes, and *Lagurus ovatus*, commonly known as hare's-tail grass, produces soft egg-shaped heads of flowers.

Bamboos These belong in a sub-family of Gramineae known as Bambusoideae, and they differ from other members of the family in that they have woody stems (hollow except for one genus), which are known as canes. Bamboos are evergreen perennials, spreading by means of rhizomes. They have lance-shaped leaves, and their flowers are not regarded as attractive. The stems die after they have flowered, but the plant itself usually survives.

RIGHT Grasses make a delightful addition to a border and an ideal foil for flowering plants such as filipendula.

BELOW LEFT A striking combination of *Cortaderia selloana* 'Sunningdale Silver', low-growing *Arundinaria viridistriata* and the striped *Miscanthus sinensis* 'Zebrinus'.

Uses in gardens Part of the grass family has a long history of cultivation, especially the cereal grasses, such as wheat, barley, oats and sweet corn, and the lawn grasses. The ornamental grasses, however, have been appreciated only in recent times, though *Cortaderia selloana* (pampas grass) and the bamboo *Arundinaria japonica* would certainly have been seen in Victorian gardens, as they were introduced into Britain in the middle of the 19th century.

During the 20th century, the number of ornamental grasses that are available has gradually increased as more have been collected from various parts of the world. A number of ornamental grasses, particularly some of those with variegated or otherwise coloured foliage, has evolved under cultivation, having been noticed and propagated by observant gardeners. It is only during the last couple of decades, however, that grasses have really caught the imagination of the gardening public.

Today, ornamental grasses are liberally used among other plants in mixed and herbaceous borders, contrasting superbly with many broad-leaved plants. But they have other uses: they are planted in gravel areas, a modern idea; highly distinctive kinds are used as isolated specimens, in lawns, perhaps, or by pools; tall grasses are used as screens; short ones make good ground cover; some are suited to tubs on a patio; and tender grasses decorate the home or conservatory.

In addition, the flowers of many, including annual kinds, are dried by flower arrangers for decoration.

Today's most popular grasses

- *Arundinaria murieliae*, Muriel bamboo
- *Cortaderia selloana*, pampas grass
- *Festuca glauca*, blue fescue
- *Helictotrichon sempervirens*, blue oat grass
- *Miscanthus sinensis* 'Zebrinus'
- *Phalaris arundinacea* var. *picta*, gardener's garters

GRASSES IN BORDERS

Ornamental perennial grasses are ideally suited to modern mixed borders, or even to herbaceous borders or island beds, as they contrast superbly with broad-leaved plants, such as shrubs and hardy perennials.

Festuca glauca continues the blue theme of this border along with *Ballota pseudodictamnus* and *Eucalyptus gunnii.*

Bluish or greyish grasses There are several perennial grasses with leaves in these colours, including *Agropyron pubiflorum*, *Festuca glauca* (blue fescue), *Helictotrichon sempervirens* (blue oat grass) and the unusual *Koeleria glauca*. These contrast particularly well with purple-leaved plants, such as the perennials *Heuchera* 'Palace Purple' and *Bergenia cordifolia* 'Purpurea', and the shrubs *Berberis thunbergii* 'Atropurpurea' and *Cotinus coggygria* 'Royal Purple'.

In addition, the bluish or greyish grasses create a superb effect when drifted or grouped around shrub roses – or indeed bush roses if these are grown in the borders – particularly if these are pink or red cultivars, which provide the best contrast.

Variegated grasses There are many perennial grasses with variegated leaves. Most are striped with green and white, creating a very light effect in borders. They include *Dactylis glomerata* 'Variegata' (cock's foot), *Holcus mollis* 'Variegatus' (variegated creeping soft grass), *Miscanthus sinensis* 'Variegatus' and *Phalaris arundinacea* var. *picta* (gardener's garters).

The 'green-and-whites' associate beautifully with many broad-leaved plants, but if you are aiming for a truly dramatic contrast, you should again try grouping them with purple-leaved plants.

Variegated grasses also make a highly effective foil for strongly-coloured perennials, such as flame-coloured crocosmias, scarlet or vermilion lychnis, or border phloxes, which often come in vibrant colours.

Then there are yellow-and-green striped grasses, particularly outstanding examples being *Alopecurus pratensis* 'Aureomarginatus' (golden foxtail), *Cortaderia selloana* 'Gold

Band' (pampas grass), *Hakonechloa macra* 'Aureola', *Miscanthus sinensis* 'Zebrinus' and *Spartina pectinata* 'Aureo Marginata'.

Again, you can achieve some dramatic contrasts by grouping these grasses with purple-leaved plants. Alternatively, adopt a more subtle approach, and create combinations that include bluish or greyish plants, such as the hostas (plantain lilies) 'Halcyon' and *H. sieboldiana* var. *elegans*, the perennial *Stachys byzantina* 'Silver Carpet', together with bluish or greyish conifers, such as *Picea pungens* 'Hoopsii' and *Chamaecyparis pisifera* 'Boulevard'.

Making the most of flowers A fairly dark, uncluttered background, such as shrubs or conifers with green foliage, is advised for grasses grown for their flowers, so that the flower heads show up really well.

Shrubs that fit the bill include *Fatsia japonica*, with its large, hand-shaped leaves, and green-leaved hollies, rhododendrons and laurels.

Among the conifers, *Cryptomeria japonica* 'Elegans', which has brownish-green foliage, and the bright-green *Chamaecyparis lawsoniana* 'Green Pillar' would make good backgrounds.

Among the best of the flowering perennial grasses that are particu-

---

Creating a sunny effect

To create a bright, sunny effect in a border, combine yellow-and-green striped grasses with golden-foliage plants – the shrubs *Philadelphus coronarius* 'Aureus' (mock orange) and *Choisya ternata* 'Sundance', for example, with hostas, such as 'Golden Medallion' and 'Gold Standard'.

---

larly recommended for mixed or herbaceous borders are *Bouteloua gracilis* (mosquito grass), *Briza media*, *Deschampsia caespitosa* 'Bronze Veil' (tufted hair grass), *Miscanthus sinensis* 'Silver Feather' and *Stipa tenacissima*.

Grasses are perfect for complementing a bright display. Here *Stipa gigantea* forms a bold clump at the front of a mixed border.

9

SPECIMENS AND SCREENS

The idea of using ornamental perennial grasses and bamboos as isolated specimens, or to form tall screens, is not new, but it is one that receives very little attention. To be used as a single isolated specimen, a grass or bamboo must be highly distinctive and have some special characteristic that one wants to show off.

The giant reed *Arundo donax* 'Versicolor' can be used as an eye-catching and unusual specimen in an island bed or lawn.

The original specimen grass for lawns must surely be *Cortaderia selloana*, pampas grass, which has attractive arching foliage and tall plumes of silvery flowers. There are several cultivars, including some suited to small gardens and others to large ones.

When growing a specimen in a lawn, be sure to leave a circle of bare soil around it, as lawn grass growing right up to the plant could retard its growth. The diameter of the circle should be in proportion to the size of the specimen and will vary from about 60–90cm (2–3ft).

The pampas grass and others may also be used as specimens at the edge of a pool, but for this to be effective a fairly large expanse of water is recommended.

Focal points Single specimen grasses and bamboos may also be used as focal points in a garden. A focal point is generally situated at the end of a vista or long view, and its purpose is to attract the eye and entice one to that part of the garden. A dramatic plant may be situated, for example, at the end or corner of a lawn, in a corner of the garden, or where a path changes direction.

Among the best grasses and bamboos for use as specimens, including those that make good focal points, are cultivars of *Arundo donax* (giant reed), *Arundinaria murieliae* (Muriel bamboo), *A. nitida* (bamboo), *Chusquea culeou* (Chilean bamboo), *Cortaderia selloana* cultivars, *Miscanthus sinensis* 'Gracillimus', *M. s.* 'Silver Feather', *Pennisetum alope-*

LEFT Bamboos grown in pots can be used as a screen or displayed as fine single specimens on the patio.

ABOVE *Miscanthus sacchariflorus* is especially striking and effective when it is grown for screening.

curoides (Chinese fountain grass), *Phyllostachys aurea* (golden bamboo), *P. bambusoides* (timber bamboo), *P. nigra* 'Boryana', *Stipa calamagrostis*, *S. gigantea*, *S. pennata* and *S. tenacissima*.

In a slightly less isolated fashion, ornamental maize or sweet corn *(Zea mays)*, which is a half-hardy annual, can be used as a dot plant in summer bedding schemes to provide height and contrast.

Screens Tall perennial grasses and bamboos make fine screens, being used mainly to hide ugly views or divide a garden rather than for wind protection, although they also help a little in this respect.

Plants for screening are simply positioned in a straight single line. For the distances at which they should be spaced, refer to the spreads given in the final section of this book. If the spread is indefinite,

space plants 45–60cm (1½–2ft) apart. To create a really dense screen, plant a double row, 45–60cm (1½–2ft) apart, staggering the plants.

The following tall grasses and bamboos are recommended for screening: *Arundinaria japonica* (arrow bamboo), *A. murieliae* (Muriel bamboo), *A. nitida* (bamboo), *Miscanthus sacchariflorus* (Amur silver grass), *Phyllostachys aurea* (golden bamboo) and *P. bambusoides*.

Specimens in tubs

Growing plants in tubs on patios is now highly popular, and some of the bamboos and grasses are excellent for this purpose. Try *Arundinaria murieliae* (Muriel bamboo), *A. nitida* (bamboo), *A. variegata* (dwarf white-stripe bamboo), *A. viridistriata* (bamboo), *Arundo donax* cultivars (giant reed) and *Hakonechloa macra* 'Aureola'.

GROUND COVER

Ground cover – the practice of completely covering the ground around larger plants, or in parts of the garden where minimum maintenance is required – is a popular gardening theme these days, and several of the perennial grasses and bamboos can be used to this effect. The idea is to cut out the necessity of weeding and cultivating the soil by completely covering the ground with low-growing plants that have a dense habit of growth. Occasionally, however, taller kinds may be preferable, provided they have a weed-smothering habit.

Preparing the site Before planting ground-cover grasses or bamboos, it is essential to ensure that the ground is completely free from weeds, especially perennials, such as couch grass, ground elder or stinging nettles.

The best way of achieving this is to spray the weeds, when they are growing vigorously, with a weed-killer containing glyphosate. If you have only annual weeds then spray these with 'Weedol'.

Rampant grasses for banks Some of the very vigorous, low-growing perennial grasses can be planted on steep banks to stabilize the soil. Their rhizomes ramify the soil and the foliage provides blanket cover, preventing the soil from becoming eroded due to rain and wind.

One of the best ornamental grasses for stabilizing banks and loose soil is the lyme grass, *Leymus arenarius*, formerly called *Elymus arenarius*. This is one of the blue grasses,

For banks or beds where a ground cover plant is desirable, the spreading *Holcus mollis* 'Variegatus' is an appealing choice.

The fine, draping growth of *Hakonechloa macra* 'Aureola' makes it an ideal grass for ground cover. It combines well with other low-growing foliage plants such as hostas.

having brilliant bluish-grey foliage.

Phalaris arundinacea var. *picta*, commonly called gardener's garters, is a highly ornamental grass with green-and-white variegated leaves. It is slightly less rampant than lyme grass, but it still needs plenty of space to spread.

Ground cover for borders The grasses and bamboos that have more restrained habits of growth make pleasing ground cover among shrubs in mixed borders, their foliage *en masse* creating very pleasing textures.

Among the variegated species, *Arundinaria variegata* (dwarf white-stripe bamboo) is especially recommended. So, too, is *Hakonechloa macra* 'Aureola', considered one of the finest of the striped grasses. *Holcus mollis* 'Variegatus' (variegated creeping soft grass) is not excessively vigorous, although it has a spreading habit. It is also recommended for covering banks.

Several bluish or greyish grasses make excellent ground cover around shrubs; *Festuca glauca*, or blue fes-

cue, for example, looks especially lovely with purple-leaved shrubs, as does the lesser-known but desirable fescue, *Festuca punctoria*.

There are several dwarf green-leaved bamboos that make attractive ground cover among shrubs, including *Sasa veitchii*. This forms dense thickets of canes and is noted for its leaf margins, which die back in autumn and become hay coloured. If taller cover is needed, you might try *Sasa tessellata*, which also forms dense thickets.

Another green-leaved bamboo is the low-growing *Shibataea kumasasa*, which is especially recommended for moist soils.

Planting distances

Grasses and bamboos for ground cover need planting reasonably close together for a quick effect. If a spread measurement is given in the section at the end of the book, this is a suitable planting distance, but if the spread is indefinite, you should set plants 30–45cm (1–1½ft) apart each way.

GRAVEL AREAS

A gravel area, in which the soil around plants is covered with a layer of gravel, is becoming a very popular feature of modern gardens, as people realize that it represents a labour-saving but very attractive way of displaying plants. Ornamental grasses are included, together with many other distinctive plants. But what is the purpose? Gravel creates a labour-saving area, as weeds cannot grow and the soil does not have to be cultivated. Gravel also makes a superb background for plants and it creates another texture, contrasting well with other surfaces such as the lawn and paving.

The combination of grasses and gravel is the basis of an easily maintained garden. Mix broad-leaved specimens with less architectural flowering plants for an integrated effect.

Choosing a site A gravel area should be sited in a sunny position with very well-drained soil.

After thoroughly preparing the soil for planting, as described on p.18, mark out any pathways through the area. These need be nothing more than well-consolidated soil, though you may choose to lay stepping stones.

After planting, cover the entire area (including soil to be used as pathways) with a 2.5–5cm (1–2in) layer of gravel. The material that is most commonly used is pea shingle, available from many builders' suppliers.

Companion plants The grasses and other plants should be positioned in informal groups, ensuring that the plants contrast well in shape, texture and colour.

There are numerous plants other than grasses that can be included, especially those kinds with sword-like leaves, such as phormiums, or New Zealand flax, and yuccas. Today there are some very colourful phormium cultivars. The yuccas produce cream or white lily-like flowers on tall stems.

Kniphofias, or red-hot pokers, are ideally suited to gravel areas. These perennials have grassy foliage and in summer produce fat spikes of flowers in shades of red, orange, yellow or cream.

Include a few plants with broader foliage, too, such as the perennial eryngiums, which produce globular heads of metallic blue flowers in summer, and *Phlomis fruticosa*, a small shrub with grey-green leaves and whorls of yellow flowers.

Choosing the grasses There are many grasses suitable for inclusion in gravel areas, but one tends to opt for those with some particularly distinctive characteristic, such as an impressive flower display.

For flowers, you might choose from the following: *Cortaderia selloana* cultivars (pampas grass), *Miscanthus sinensis* 'Silver Feather', *Stipa calamagrostis*, *S. gigantea*, *S. pennata* and *S. tenacissima*.

A selection of grasses that are suitable for a gravel area and have attractive foliage could include *Agropyron pubiflorum*, *Festuca glauca* (blue fescue), *F. punctoria* and *Sesleria heufleriana*, all dwarf grasses for a frontal position; and the taller *Helictotrichon sempervirens* (blue oat grass), *Miscanthus*

sacchariflorus (Amur silver grass), *M. sinensis* 'Gracillimus', *M. s.* 'Variegatus', *M. s.* 'Zebrinus' and *Spartina pectinata* 'Aureo Marginata' (but do not subject the last to very dry conditions).

An effective group

The following plants combine effectively: *Kniphofia* 'Little Maid' (a red-hot poker with spikes of cream-yellow flowers), *Helictotrichon sempervirens* and *Phormium* 'Cream Delight' (a New Zealand flax, with leaves that have a wide cream central band).

ABOVE The distinctive striped leaves of *Glyceria maxima* 'Variegata' contrast well with stones and gravel.

LEFT A bamboo makes a good focal point in a small gravelled area.

ANNUAL GRASSES

Annuals are plants with a life cycle (germination of the seed through to flowering, seed setting and death) that is completed during one growing season. Surprisingly, perhaps, annual grasses are not as widely grown as the perennials, yet they are easily raised from seeds, generally sown in the open ground, and they flower prolifically, which is their main virtue. Flower arrangers love them because the flowers of most species, produced in summer, can be dried and used in dried-flower arrangements to brighten up the winter months.

The feathery flower heads of *Hordeum jubatum* are a delightful asset to any garden.

Which to grow There are several very well-known and a few unusual annual grasses, all highly distinctive in habit. One of the more unusual species is the hardy *Agrostis nebulosa* (cloud grass), which has dainty cloud-like sprays of flowers.

Briza maxima (greater quaking grass) is one of the better-known hardy annuals, prized for its dangling oval flowers.

Not too well known, but deserving to be more widely grown, is the hardy *Bromus macrostachys* (Mediterranean brome grass) which has relatively large flowers for an annual grass.

The well-loved *Coix lacryma-jobi* (Job's tears) is a half-hardy annual with attractive bead-like seeds. This particular annual grass is not normally dried for arrangements.

The hardy *Hordeum jubatum* (foxtail barley) is prized for its highly decorative feathery flowers. *Lagurus ovatus* (hare's-tail grass), another hardy grass, is equally valued, producing soft white egg-shaped heads of flowers.

Not too well known is the halfhardy annual *Setaria glauca* (yellow bristle grass), which has long spikelike heads of reddish-gold bristly flowers. The ornamental cultivars of *Zea mays* (ornamental maize or sweet corn) are also half-hardy annuals, in this case grown mainly for their attractive variegated or striped foliage.

Where to grow annuals Annual grasses are suitable for mixed borders, where they can, for example, be associated with shrubs. Dark-leaved shrubs, including those with deep purple foliage, provide an excellent background for the flowers.

The annual grasses, being rather subdued in colour, can also be combined effectively with brightly-coloured hardy perennials in a mixed border. For example, many of the border phloxes have strongly-coloured, perhaps even strident, flowers, and these grasses help to tone the more brilliant pinks down.

Annual grasses can also be mixed with other hardy or half-hardy annuals, especially brightly-coloured kinds such as *Alonsoa warscewitczii* (mask flower), with its bright red flowers, the rose-red *Linum grandiflorum* (annual flax) and deep orange-red *Tithonia rotundifolia* (Mexican sunflower).

Annuals with daisy-like flowers

that also make good companions for grasses include the rose-pink *Helipterum roseum* or *Acroclinium roseum* (Australian everlasting), *Helichrysum bracteatum* (strawflower) in mixed bright colours, and *Xeranthemum annuum* (immortelle) in pink, lilac and white, all of which are suitable subjects for drying.

Intermingled with other plants, annual grasses look good in patio beds or borders, where they contrast beautifully with paving.

The ornamental maize or sweet corn is generally used to create height in summer bedding schemes and is especially suitable for subtropical bedding, combining well with such exotics as *Ricinus communis* (the castor-oil plant) and *Canna* (Indian shot).

If you want lots of grasses for cutting and drying, it may be better to grow them in rows in the vegetable garden, to prevent ruining the displays in the borders when they are cut for indoor use.

BELOW The resplendent leaves of *Zea mays* 'Gigantea Quadricolor'.

ABOVE RIGHT *Bromus macrostachys*, one of the less common annual grasses.

CULTIVATION

Perennial and annual grasses require very little attention. They need to be planted correctly, however, and in suitable conditions, and like other plants, they require feeding and watering. The stems of herbaceous kinds need cutting down annually. Fortunately, in contrast to many other plants, grasses are troubled by few pests and diseases.

Aspect Most grasses need a sunny position, but a few will grow in shade, and this is indicated, where appropriate, in the descriptions at the end of the book.

Bamboos will tolerate partial shade and should be sheltered from cold winds. Generally, other grasses, provided they are hardy, do not mind wind.

Soil preferences Grasses are very tolerant of soils and will grow in any type, provided the drainage is good. Few will tolerate wet or waterlogged conditions, although some need constantly moist soil. Bamboos grow best in soils that do not tend to dry out.

Preparation Before planting perennial grasses or sowing annuals, it pays to prepare the soil thoroughly to promote optimum growth.

First ensure that the planting site is completely free from weeds, especially perennial kinds (including perennial weed grasses), as these are almost impossible to control when established among ornamental grasses. The best way to control perennial weeds is to spray them while in active growth with glyphosate weedkiller. If you only have annual weeds, spray them with 'Weedol'.

When weeds are dead, carry out the digging. Deep or double digging (to two depths of the spade) may be

LEFT A healthy flowering *Setaria italica*, a half-hardy annual grass. Provided they are planted in well-prepared soil in a suitably sunny position, most grasses require little attention.

RIGHT Bamboos are ideal for areas in partial shade, such as the corner of a patio.

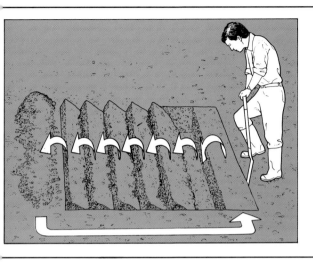

Double digging Dig a row one spade blade deep and wide, and loosen soil beneath this trench to a further spade depth. Dig a row behind in the same manner, throwing this soil into the first trench. Continue in this way until the plot is dug over, filling in the final row with the soil from the first one.

necessary if the soil is not well drained. This will improve drainage, especially if plenty of grit or coarse sand is incorporated – add it to the trenches and also mix it with the top layer of soil. If drainage is acceptable, single digging will be sufficient.

Bulky organic matter should be

added to the trenches when you dig. You can use 'Forest Bark' Ground and Composted Bark, well-rotted garden compost, spent mushroom compost, or spent hops or peat substitutes. Bulky organic matter assists the drainage of heavy soils and conversely helps light dry types to retain more moisture.

Just before planting, apply a base dressing of a balanced granular flower-garden fertilizer, according to the instructions on the pack, to get the plants off to a good start.

Planting To ensure that they establish themselves rapidly, ornamental grasses are best planted in mid-spring, when the soil is warming up and drying out. If the soil is of a very well-drained type, such as a light sand, then mid-autumn planting could be undertaken, but only for herbaceous perennials. Evergreen grasses (including the bamboos) are best planted in spring.

Grasses will resent being planted too deeply. Plant them to the same depth that they were growing previously, with the crown (where the growth buds are) at soil level.

When planting a container-grown grass from a garden centre, cover the top of the rootball with only 12mm (½in) of soil. On no account should the rootball be disturbed, so remove the container carefully. Make the hole slightly larger than the rootball, position the plant centrally in it, then work fine soil into the space between the rootball and the sides of the hole.

If you are planting a grass without soil around its roots, dig a hole sufficiently deep to allow the roots to dangle straight down without turning up at their ends, then work fine soil around them.

The soil should be well firmed around grasses, which is easily accomplished by treading all round with your heel.

Feeding Ornamental grasses and bamboos should be fed only sparingly; if you overfeed, they could make very lush soft growth, which is more likely to be damaged by weather and attacked by mildew.

A balanced granular flower-garden fertilizer, applied as a top-dressing in spring each year, according to the instructions on the pack, and lightly forked into the soil surface, will be sufficient for perennial grasses. The base dressing that is given prior to sowing should be sufficient for annual grasses. Feed the latter too much, and they may produce lots of vegetative growth at the expense of flowers.

A balanced fertilizer contains nitrogen, phosphorus and potash, which are the three most important plant

With a container-grown grass, do not disturb the rootball when planting. Place in a hole slightly larger than the rootball and fill in carefully.

For plants that do not have soil around their roots, dig a hole deep enough for the roots to hang straight down, and work fine soil around them.

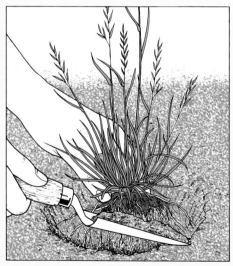

Grasses add autumn interest to a garden, and associate well with late-flowering plants such as *Sedum spectabile* and *Polygonum amplexicaule.*

foods. Nitrogen is especially important for grasses – but not in excessive doses – as it promotes the growth of foliage and stems. Potash promotes flowering, while phosphorus ensures good root development.

Watering Ornamental grasses, including bamboos, will benefit from being watered if the soil becomes dry in the spring or summer. Certainly those kinds that need or appreciate moist soil should not be allowed to become dry.

Obviously, you should water the entire border or bed if necessary, and this is best accomplished with a garden sprinkler. It is important to apply enough water each time, aiming to keep the top 15cm (6in) moist during dry weather.

To achieve this, you must apply about 27 litres of water per square metre (almost 5 gallons per square yard). This equals 2.5cm (1in) of rain, which can be measured by standing empty tin cans under the sprinkler to catch the falling water.

Tidying up The dead stems of herbaceous perennial grasses should be cut down to the ground annually. This can be done in the autumn as soon as they have completely died down; or it can be delayed until the beginning or middle of spring the following year, as the dead, hay-coloured stems of many grasses have a decorative value. Any dead leaves on evergreen grasses can also be removed in the spring by cutting as close to the ground as possible.

Troubles

Fortunately, ornamental grasses are troubled by few pests and diseases.
- Powdery mildew – white or brownish fungal patches on lower leaves; grey-white mould can cover the whole plant. Spray with Benlate + 'Activex' 2. Avoid heavy applications of nitrogenous fertilizer.
- Rabbits – these eat young shoots and foliage. Use an animal repellant.

PROPAGATION

Ornamental perennial grasses, including bamboos, are generally propagated by division. Some, however, can be raised from seed, which is also the method for annual grasses.

It is a simple task to divide clump-forming grasses like *Agropyron pubiflorum*, here making a fine edging to a border.

Division The perennial ornamental grasses, including bamboos, are propagated by division in mid-spring. At this time, the soil is warming up and drying out and therefore the divisions quickly become established.

Division also keeps the plants young and vigorous, so it is a good idea to lift and divide perennial grasses every three or four years. It is not the usual practice, though, to lift and divide bamboos regularly, and this should only be done when you want to increase them.

To divide an established clump, lift it carefully with a garden fork and shake off as much soil as possible. Not all grass clumps are tough, and some can easily be pulled apart by hand. The clumps of certain grasses, however, and certainly those of bamboos, will be very solid, so the best way to divide these is to thrust two garden forks back to back through the clump and then prise the handles apart to split the clump in two. Divide these two portions in the same way, and then divide again if necessary. Portions approximately 15cm (6in) in diameter are the ideal size for replanting.

When dividing plants, always discard the centre of each; this is the oldest part, and declining in vigour. Retain for replanting only the young vigorous outer parts of each clump.

Replant divisions as described for bare-root plants under Planting on the preceding pages.

Raising plants from seed Species of hardy perennial grasses (not cultivars) can be raised from seed sown in an outdoor seed bed during mid-spring. Make sure the soil is well drained and raked down to a fine tilth. Sow thinly in rows and cover lightly with fine soil.

As soon as the seedlings are large enough to handle easily, transplant them to a nursery bed to give them room to grow. They can be spaced about 15cm (6in) apart each way. When you consider that they are sufficiently large, plant into permanent positions; this will generally be in mid-spring the following year.

Hardy annual grasses are also sown during mid-spring, but in this case they are sown where they are to flower. Mark out bold informal or irregular patches and then sow the seeds in rows across them, about 15cm (6in) apart. This is better than broadcast sowing and makes weeding and the thinning of surplus seedlings much easier. Thin out seedlings, if necessary, so that they stand about 15cm (6in) apart.

Half-hardy annual grasses can either be sown outdoors, in late spring, or started off under glass during early spring.

Under glass, sow the seeds thinly in seed trays, using a well-drained soil-based seed compost; cover lightly with compost, and germinate the seeds in a temperature of 15.5°C (60°F). Transplant seedlings into further trays, using a well-drained soil-based potting compost. Harden the seeds in a garden frame for two weeks, then plant them out in late spring or early summer, when all danger of frost is over.

There are some special sowing tips for *Zea mays*, the ornamental maize or sweet corn, under that entry on p.47 at the end of this book.

LEFT To divide large grass clumps in two, insert two garden forks back to back into the centre of the clump and prise the handles apart. You can repeat this process with the halved clumps until they are of the desired size for replanting.

BELOW To prick out grass seedlings, ease them carefully out of the seed pan with a plant label. Hold them by a leaf (never by the stem), and transfer them to prepared holes made with a dibber in small pots or further trays, firming the soil lightly around them.

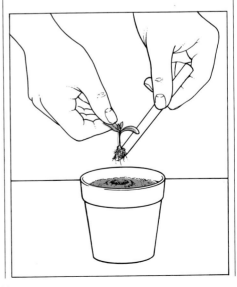

GRASSES INDOORS

Some tender grasses are grown as houseplants or conservatory plants, while several hardy bamboos can be used inside for decorative purposes, but only for short spells.

Oplismenus hirtellus 'Variegatus' is an indoor grass with a trailing habit which makes it ideal for hanging baskets or other raised containers.

Tender grasses Two grasses of creeping habit are grown as house-plants or conservatory plants: *Oplismenus hirtellus* 'Variegatus', with green-and-white striped leaves, and the green-and-cream striped *Stenotaphrum secundatum* 'Variegatum' (variegated St Augustine grass).

Due to their habit of growth, both can be grown in hanging baskets or other elevated containers, and they are also useful either for edging the staging in a conservatory or for window-sill cultivation, as they will grow down over the edge.

These grasses need a minimum temperature of 13°C (56°F), and they associate well with other house or conservatory plants that require a similar environment. These include the flowering pot plant *Celosia cristata*, which has brightly-coloured feathery flower heads, fuchsias and *Pelargonium domesticum* (regal pelargonium), as well as colourful foliage plants such as *Coleus* (flame nettles), with their multicoloured leaves, and *Hypoestes phyllostachya* (polka dot plant), which is splashed and spotted with pink.

Provide bright light, but shade plants from strong sun; *Oplismenus*, in fact, prefers partial shade. The plants should be watered well during the growing season, but far less generously in winter, when you should allow the compost to dry out to a certain extent. Both these grasses are best grown in a very well-drained soil-based potting compost.

If you want to create a really attractive effect in a hanging basket, plant up to 10 rooted cuttings in it, depending on the size of the basket. Both grasses should be propagated frequently, as young plants look more attractive than older ones.

Plants can be fed monthly with a

liquid houseplant food such as 'Kerigrow'. Overfeeding, however, leads to very lush, soft and untypical growth, so be careful not to overdo it.

Arundo donax (giant reed) and its cultivars 'Macrophylla' and 'Versicolor' are half hardy and intolerant of temperatures below 0°C (32°F). Unless you live in a frost-free climate, it is therefore a good idea to grow this grass in a tub, so that you are able to move it into a frost-free greenhouse or conservatory during the winter. During the summer it could be placed on a patio. Being an herbaceous grass it will not, unfortunately, contribute to the plant display while under glass.

Hardy bamboos for indoors Some of the hardy bamboos can be grown in tubs and used for indoor display, either in the house or in a conservatory. Large plants are generally used as single specimens and make fine and unusual focal points; use one, for example, to create an exotic atmosphere in a room.

They should not, however, be kept inside longer than a week at a time, especially inside the house, as they do not really like these conditions. If you keep a bamboo plant in a room for a while, allow it to recuperate outdoors afterwards. You might, perhaps, use it for a special occasion, such as a dinner party. Of course, bamboos in tubs are also ideal for decorating the patio.

The more graceful species of bamboo are recommended for indoor display, especially *Arundinaria murieliae* (Muriel bamboo) and its new cultivar 'Simba'. *A. nitida* is also well worth considering. If you want more colour, opt for *A. viridistriata*, which has yellow-striped leaves.

For tub culture, bamboos are best grown in a well-drained soil-based potting compost.

BELOW The tumbling *Stenotaphrum secundatum* 'Variegatum' is an elegant camouflage for staging in the greenhouse or conservatory.

BOTTOM Tub-grown bamboos can be brought indoors for brief periods to make a very effective focal point in a room, but must go back outside after a few days.

SIXTY OF THE BEST

Here is a guide to 60 of the best perennial and annual grasses, including bamboos. All of them are available: most can be found in general hardy-plant nurseries, and a few are normally on offer at garden centres. Some, though, will have to be purchased as seeds from seedsmen, and this applies mainly to the annual grasses.

Agropyron pubiflorum
(A. magellanicum)

This is not a rampant weed grass (that's *Agropyron repens* or couch grass). This is a perfectly restrained hardy perennial clump-forming grass, about 30cm (1ft) high with a similar spread. It is a comparatively recent arrival, and possibly the brightest of the grasses with silver-blue leaves. Ideal for borders or gravel areas, it contrasts superbly with many other broad-leaved plants, and thrives in sun or shade.

Agrostis nebulosa

Cloud grass is a tufted hardy annual grass, about 30cm (1ft) high and with a spread of about 15cm (6in). The leaves are green, and have a rough texture. The dainty sprays of flowers, produced in midsummer, are very attractive and can be dried.

Alopecurus pratensis
'Aureomarginatus'

(*A.p.* 'Aureo-variegatus', *A.p.* 'Aureus')
Golden foxtail is a hardy herbaceous perennial grass, forming tufts of leaves that are striped with yellow and green. The densely-packed flower spikes are attractive in summer. Golden foxtail has a height and spread of up to 30cm (1ft), and is recommended for edging borders.

Arrhenatherum elatius 'Variegatum'

False oat grass is a tufted hardy herbaceous perennial with grey-green leaves, edged with white, and conspicuous heads of brown flowers in summer. The bases of the stems are swollen and look like bulbs. The plant has a height of 45cm (1½ft) and a spread of some 20cm (8in). A dark-leaved shrub would make a good background for this grass.

Alopecurus pratensis 'Aureomarginatus' makes an attractive border plant

ABOVE *Arundinaria murieliae*
RIGHT *Arundinaria nitida*

Arundinaria japonica
(Pseudosasa japonica)
Also called either arrow bamboo or metake, this is a commonly-grown and extremely hardy bamboo, forming a dense clump of olive-green canes. The broad lance-shaped evergreen leaves are at least 30cm (1ft) in length, and the plant reaches a height of 4.5m (15ft), with an indefinite spread. This bamboo can be used for screening.

Arundinaria murieliae
*(Thamnocalamus spathaceus,
Sinarundinaria murieliae)*
Muriel bamboo is a moderately hardy evergreen which has been burdened with some awful names, but it is one of the most attractive bamboos for the garden. Clump-forming in habit, with yellow-green canes, it bears bright-green leaves with long pointed tips. It has a height of 3.6m (12ft), with an indefinite spread, and is ideal for borders, specimen planting or screening, and very suitable for growing in a tub on the patio. A new cultivar – a rare occurence with bamboos – was introduced in 1990. Called 'Simba', it has a graceful, arching yet compact habit of growth. It attains only about 1.8m (6ft) in height.

Arundinaria nitida
(Sinarundinaria nitida)
Another moderately hardy and very elegant evergreen bamboo, this forms clumps of purple-flushed canes that carry small medium-green leaves with pointed tips. It has a height of 4.5m (15ft), with an indefinite spread. Best grown in partial shade, this bamboo makes a fine specimen or screen and is amenable to tub culture.

Arundinaria variegata
(A. fortunei, Pleioblastus variegatus)
Dwarf white-stripe bamboo makes ideal ground cover, although it spreads only slowly. Moderately hardy, it contrasts well with shrubs in a border, and is ideal for tubs. The narrow evergreen leaves are boldly striped with green and white. The canes produce branches, and the plant reaches a height of 76cm (2½ft), with an indefinite spread.

Arundinaria viridistriata
(A. auricoma, Pleioblastus viridis-triatus)
One of the most colourful bamboos, this has purple canes carrying broad evergreen leaves of bright yellow striped with green. Moderately hardy, it spreads slowly, reaching a height of 1.5m (5ft), with an indefinite spread. It is recommended for borders, placed with shrubs, and is ideal for tubs. New canes have the best colour, so to encourage these the old ones can be cut down in autumn.

Arundo donax 'Macrophylla'
The giant reed is a tall herbaceous perennial grass, with wide, arching blue-green leaves that are borne on fat stems of the same colour. Yellowish-white flowers are carried in dense heads during summer. This reed can reach a height of up to 3.6m (12ft), with a spread of 60cm (2ft), and is a superb specimen plant.

Arundo donax 'Versicolor'

Unfortunately, it is only half hardy, and is intolerant of temperatures below freezing. It is therefore best grown in a tub and wintered in a frost-free greenhouse or conservatory. It requires moist soil.

Arundo donax 'Versicolor'
(A.d. 'Variegata')
Another variety of giant reed, this is similar to *A.d.* 'Macrophylla' except that the broad leaves are boldly striped with green and cream. It reaches a height of up to 3m (10ft), with a spread of 60cm (2ft).

Bouteloua gracilis
(B. oligostachya)
Mosquito grass, also known as blue grama, is a hardy tuft-forming grass that is partially evergreen. The green leaves are very narrow, but the main attraction lies in its brown, bristly, one-sided flower spikes. Produced in summer, these are suitable for drying. This grass has a height of 45cm (1½ft), with a spread of 20cm (8in), and is ideal for borders.

Bouteloua gracilis

The dainty flowers of *Briza maxima*

Briza maxima
Greater quaking grass is a vigorous, very hardy annual grass, forming tufts of medium-green leaves. It is grown primarily for its dainty sprays of pendulous oval green-purple flowers, which are produced in early summer. These are ideal for drying for indoor arrangements. The tufts have a height of 45cm (1½ft), with a spread of 10cm (4in).

Briza media
Commonly known as common quaking grass, this is a very hardy perennial grass that forms tufts of medium-green evergreen leaves. It is grown mainly for its sprays of purple-brown, dangling, heart-shaped flowers, which are produced in summer, and are excellent for drying. This grass reaches a height of up to 60cm (2ft), with a spread of 10cm (4in).

Bromus macrostachys
Mediterranean brome grass is a hardy annual, grown for its comparatively large flowers. These appear in early summer and are excellent for drying. The grass has a height of 30–60cm (1–2ft), with a spread of about 10cm (4in).

Chusquea culeou
Chilean bamboo is a very exotic-looking plant with solid (as opposed to hollow) dark-green canes. These have swollen joints, or nodes, with white sheaths, from which clusters of slender side branches are produced. The evergreen leaves, which are small and have slender points, are mid-green. This very hardy species forms dense clumps, but is slow growing. It reaches a height of up to 4.5m (15ft), with a spread of at least 2.4m (8ft), and is excellent as a focal point or specimen.

Coix lacryma-jobi has bead-like seeds

Coix lacryma-jobi

Job's tears is a half-hardy annual grass with tufts of quite distinctive broad light-green foliage. The flowers are not particularly conspicuous, the seeds being much more attractive. These are bead-like – indeed, they can be used as beads – and appear in autumn, turning to a greyish-mauve colour when ripe. The plant has a height of 45–90cm (1½–3ft), with a spread of up to 15cm (6in).

Cortaderia selloana 'Gold Band'

Pampas grass is a hardy perennial, in this cultivar forming a clump of narrow arching evergreen foliage, variegated golden-yellow and green. The plumes of silvery flowers that are produced in summer reach a height of 1.5m (5ft), and the plant spreads to about 90cm (3ft). It is excellent for borders, where it contrasts well with many shrubs, and is equally useful for gravel areas and for specimen planting.

C. s. 'Pumila'

This cultivar of pampas grass forms a clump about 90cm (3ft) across, with narrow, arching green foliage and, in late summer, plumes of silvery flowers that reach a height of 1.5m (5ft). 'Pumila' is ideal for specimen planting or for use as a focal point in the smaller garden. It also looks superb by a pool, especially when planted with shrubs noted for autumn leaf colour, and it is excellent for gravel areas.

C. s. 'Sunningdale Silver'

A larger version of *C.s.* 'Pumila', this has the same uses and is therefore suitable for the larger garden. The plumes are cream-white and rise to a height of 2.1m (7ft), and the plant has a spread of 1.2m (4ft).

Dactylis glomerata 'Variegata'

Known as cock's foot or orchard grass, this is a hardy perennial grass that forms a tuft of evergreen foliage. It is attractively striped with grey green and silver and contrasts well with shrubs and broad-leaved perennials that have dark-green foliage; it also contrasts well with purple-leaved shrubs. Sprays of attractive purple-green flowers are produced in summer. The plant has a height of 90cm (3ft), with a spread up to 25cm (10in).

Deschampsia caespitosa 'Bronze Veil'

Tufted hair grass is a highly distinctive grass in both foliage and flower. A very hardy evergreen perennial, it forms a tuft of narrow dark-green leaves. Delicate sprays of bronze flowers, resembling a fountain, are produced during the summer and last for a long period. This grass prefers to grow in moist soil and tolerates very acid conditions. It has a height of up to 1.2m (4ft), with a spread of approximately 45cm (1½ft). It can look very attractive in borders, as it associates well with shrubs and other broad-leaved plants. A superb effect is achieved, when the grass is in flower, if it has been planted with a silver-foliage shrub such as *Elaeagnus commutata*, the silver berry.

Deschampsia flexuosa 'Tetragold'

Wavy hair grass is a tufted hardy perennial with very narrow spiky leaves, which are yellow in the spring but then change to a bright yellow green in the summer. This is a relatively new and little-known cultivar, attaining a height and spread of about 22cm (9in). Ideal for planting in bold groups or drifts at the front of a border, it associates well with many other plants, such as purple-leaved berberis and *Stachys byzantina* 'Silver Carpet', which forms mats of grey woolly leaves.

Cortaderia selloana 'Pumila'

Deschampsia flexuosa 'Tetragold'

Festuca glauca 'Blue-glow', a popular blue grass

Festuca glauca

Blue fescue is one of the most popular of the 'blue-leaved' grasses and should be in every garden, where it associates beautifully with many plants. Try growing it, for example, with purple-leaved plants, such as the hardy perennial *Heuchera* 'Palace Purple'. It also associates well with paving, so it could be planted in a patio bed or border, and it contrasts equally well with gravel. The blue fescue also makes effective ground cover around shrubs, such as purple-leaved berberis. It is a hardy tuft-forming species with thin spiky evergreen foliage, varying in colour from blue green to a silvery white, the flowers being blue green. The plant has a height and spread of 15cm (6in). There are several new named forms with improved foliage colour; these include 'Silver Sea' (silver blue) and 'Blue-glow' (an intense silver blue).

Festuca punctoria

Fescue is a hardy clump-forming evergreen perennial, producing

Glyceria maxima 'Variegata'

Hakonechloa macra 'Aureola', an adaptable striped grass

rigid, curved and rolled, bright grey-green leaves with sharp tips, giving a somewhat spiky effect. The flowers are greyish. Fescue has a height and spread of about 15cm (6in), and is excellent for planting in bold groups at the front of a border or for use as contrasting ground cover around broad-leaved shrubs. It looks striking against gravel and paving.

Glyceria maxima 'Variegata'
(*G. aquatica* 'Variegata')
Reed meadow grass, or reed sweet, is one of the few grasses that prefer moist soil. Indeed, this particular grass is an excellent subject for planting in wet conditions at the edge of a pool, although it will grow almost as well in a border that has moisture-retentive soil. This hardy herbaceous perennial grass has a spreading habit of growth. The long arching leaves are conspicuously striped with cream and green, their bases often being flushed with pink. During the summer, graceful sprays of greenish flowers are produced, but the main attraction is the foliage.

This attractive grass reaches a height of 76cm (2½ft), with an indefinite spread.

Hakonechloa macra 'Aureola'
This is one of the finest of the striped grasses, forming a clump of arching foliage that resembles a low fountain in shape. The leaves are striped with bright yellow and green, but this colour changes to reddish brown as the leaves age. In early summer, sprays of red-brown flowers may be produced, and these remain attractive throughout the winter months. This hardy herbaceous perennial grass is slow growing, reaching a height of 45cm (1½ft) and a spread of 45–60cm (1½–2ft). *Hakonechloa macra* needs a reasonably moist soil, and is excellent for use in a border, contrasting with many plants, such as blue or grey conifers, grey or blue hostas and *Bergenia cordifolia* 'Purpurea', which has purple-flushed foliage. This adaptable grass can be used as ground cover if desired, and is also suitable for growing in a tub on a patio.

Helictotrichon sempervirens
(Avena candida, A. sempervirens)
Blue oat grass is equally as popular as *Festuca glauca*, if not more so, but is a larger plant. A hardy evergreen perennial, with a tufted habit of growth, it produces stiff spiky silver-blue leaves, about 30cm (1ft) in length. In the summer, pale yellowish flowers appear, but they are not especially attractive. The plant has an overall height of 90cm (3ft), with a spread of 60cm (2ft). Blue oat grass is suitable for borders, associating with many broad-leaved plants. When planted in bold groups or drifts, it makes a particularly good companion for shrub roses. This grass contrasts superbly with paving, so it can be recommended for patio beds or borders and it also looks attractive in gravel areas, making an excellent companion for plants with broader, sword-like foliage, such as phormiums and yuccas.

Helictotrichon sempervirens

The splendid evergreen *Holcus mollis* 'Variegatus'

Hordeum jubatum produces distinctive flower spikes

Holcus mollis 'Variegatus'

Variegated creeping soft grass is striped with green and white, and is dwarf and very hardy. The species itself is a weed, but this attractive cultivar has a spreading habit of growth, making good ground cover, especially as it is evergreen. Try planting this grass among shrubs in a border, especially those with purple foliage. Alternatively, it would make good cover for a bank. When planted in a mass, it creates an almost white effect. The flowers are purplish-white and are produced during the summer, but they are not very attractive – this is essentially a foliage plant. It reaches a height of 30–45cm (1–1½ft), with an indefinite spread.

Hordeum jubatum

Foxtail barley, or squirrel-tail grass as it is also known, is a hardy annual of tufted habit, which is grown for its highly decorative flower spikes. Overall the colour of pale hay, these arching, feathery spikes are produced during the summer and early autumn, and can be dried for use in winter decorations. The foxtail barley grows to a height of 30–60cm (1–2ft) and has a spread of 30cm (1ft). This grass looks most attractive when planted in a mixed border, especially when it is given a dark background, such as a deep-green shrub, to offset its flowers. The foxtail barley also looks lovely with brightly-coloured perennials, such as border phloxes. It also looks good around the edges of patio beds and borders, as the flowers contrast well with paving. In this situation, it makes a good combination with some brightly-coloured annuals, such as the red-flowered flax, *Linum grandiflorum* 'Rubrum'.

Lagurus ovatus is grown for its pretty summer and autumn flowers

Koeleria glauca

This unusual and very hardy perennial grass deserves to become much better known. It has attractive grey-green foliage and is useful for mixed borders, where it contrasts well with many plants. It is grown for its foliage rather than its flowers, which are produced in summer. Of compact habit, the plants reach a height of about 45cm (1½ft), with a spread of approximately 30cm (1ft).

Lagurus ovatus

Known as hare's-tail grass, this is a very distinctive hardy annual of tufted habit, and is grown for the large, soft, white egg-shaped heads of flowers. The flowers, about 38mm (1½in) in length, are produced early on in the summer, but they last until well into the autumn, and they can be dried for winter use. The flat grey-green hairy leaves are quite long and narrow, but are not espe-

cially attractive. Hare's-tail grass, which reaches a height of 45cm (1½ft), with a spread of 15cm (6in), can be grown in mixed borders, but it would also look effective in patio beds and other borders. In either case, it combines well with brightly-coloured annuals or perennials.

Leymus arenarius

(Elymus arenarius)

Here we have a peculiar name change, for the lyme grass was until recently known as elymus. Whatever the name, this is one of the most beautiful of the blue grasses, but it should carry a warning: it is extremely rampant, and you should not risk allowing it into your garden unless you have plenty of space to devote to it, or it may swamp nearby plants. In practice, its main use is for stabilizing soil on banks, for which task it is supreme. It is ideal ground cover for coastal areas, too, binding light sandy soil or sand dunes. Ideal companion plants would include maritime shrubs, such as pink-flowered tamarisk. Lyme grass is a very hardy herbaceous perennial, spreading by means of rhizomes. The wide leaves, 60cm (2ft) or more in length, are a brilliant bluish-grey and create a marvellous texture *en masse*. When in flower, which occurs during the summer, this grass is about 1.5m (5ft) high. The spread is indefinite.

Melica ciliata

Silky-spike melic, or pearl grass, is an unusual hardy perennial grass, which is grown for its stiff erect flower spikes. These are 15cm (6in) long, appearing during the first half of summer, and are excellent subjects for drying for winter decoration. They are bright brown, decorated with long silver-white silky hairs, and are carried on slender stems. The greyish-green leaves, which are narrow or rolled, are rather stiff. Pearl grass has a height of about 60cm (2ft), with a spread of about half this. This grass is normally sold as seed in Britain, but this is no problem as they are easily raised. It is an excellent grass for the mixed border, especially in association with shrubs, and deserves to become better known.

Melica ciliata

Leymus arenarius, a fast-spreading blue grass

Milium effusum 'Aureum'

Golden wood millet is one of the best of the golden grasses, the flat leaves, up to 30cm (1ft) long, being a rich golden yellow. It is a hardy dwarf evergreen perennial with a tufted habit of growth. In summer it produces greeny-yellow flowers, but these are not particularly attractive, golden wood millet being essentially a foliage plant. In flower, it reaches a height of 90cm (3ft), and it has a spread of 30cm (1ft). It self-sows quite freely, so be careful not to disturb any small seedlings when you cultivate around the plants. The golden wood millet is best grown in shade with reasonably moist soil, where it associates well with such plants as blue or grey hostas, ferns, bergenias and primroses.

Miscanthus sacchariflorus

Called Amur silver grass, this is one of the largest perennial grasses, but it is of moderate hardiness and rarely produces flowers in Britain. This species is herbaceous and grows vigorously, sending up stems to a height of about 3m (10ft) each year. It has an indefinite spread, increasing slowly by means of rhizomes. The long, broad arching leaves are mid-green and last well into winter.

This grass makes an excellent screen, for which purpose plants should be set 45–60cm (1½–2ft) apart. An individual plant can be allowed to form a sizeable clump towards the back of a mixed border, where it will associate well with broad-leaved shrubs. Another effective setting for this grass is a gravel area, especially if this is associated with architectural features.

Miscanthus sinensis 'Gracillimus'

A moderately hardy herbaceous perennial grass of clump-forming habit, this has very narrow dark-

Milium effusum 'Aureum'

Miscanthus sinensis 'Silver Feather'

green leaves. Sometimes, sprays of white flowers are produced at the beginning of autumn, but one cannot rely on flowers and in any case this is essentially a foliage plant. With a height of 1.2m (4ft) and a spread of 45cm (1½ft), this is a beautiful grass for the mixed border or gravel area, where it is at its best when combined with plants that have coloured foliage, such as purple or yellow phormiums. It also makes a good specimen or focal point.

M. s. 'Silver Feather'
This moderately hardy herbaceous perennial, which is of clump-forming habit, is grown for its spectacular autumn flower display. It produces light silvery-brown plumes to a height of nearly 2.4m (8ft), and it also has long, arching green foliage. This grass can be grown in a mixed border, perhaps with shrubs noted for autumn leaf colour or berries, or as a specimen in a lawn or by a pool. It is also highly recommended for use in a gravel area.

M. s. 'Variegatus'
A moderately hardy clump-forming herbaceous perennial grass, the leaves of which are striped with cream and green, this is grown for its foliage. It reaches a height of up to 1.2m (4ft), with a spread of 45–60cm (1½–2ft). A useful addition to a mixed border, where it can be situated in association with shrubs, and it also looks most attractive when used in gravel areas.

M. s. 'Zebrinus'
This is the most popular of the *M. s.* cultivars and one of the most distinctive, the leaves having cream cross bands. This grass is a moderately hardy herbaceous perennial, forming a clump. Sprays of white flowers may be produced during autumn, but the main attraction is the foliage. Plants reach a height of 1.2m (4ft), with a spread of 45–60cm (1½–2ft). *M. s.* 'Zebrinus' is ideal for mixed borders, where it is grown in association with shrubs, and is also recommended for gravel areas.

Miscanthus sinensis 'Variegatus' provides attractive foliage

Oplismenus hirtellus 'Variegatus'

Pennisetum alopecuroides 'Woodside'

Molinia caerulea 'Variegata'

Variegated purple moor grass is one of the most popular small variegated grasses, its leaves being striped with green and yellow. Sprays of purple flowers (hence the common name) are produced towards the end of the summer. It is a clump-forming hardy herbaceous perennial, attaining a height of 60cm (2ft), with a spread of about 30cm (1ft). Try planting it in bold groups in a mixed border, perhaps with purple-leaved shrubs or perennials.

Oplismenus hirtellus 'Variegatus'

This grass is used as a houseplant or conservatory plant as it is tender, requiring a minimum temperature of 13°C (56°F). An evergreen perennial of creeping habit, the stems root at their joints into the soil. The leaves, which are lance shaped with long, pointed tips, are boldly striped with green and white and generally flushed with pink. This grass has a height of at least 20cm (8in), and an indefinite spread. It should be grown in partial shade and provided with a well-drained soil-based potting compost. Thanks to its trailing habit, it can be grown to good effect in a hanging basket or other elevated container, or allowed to trail over a window-sill or the edge of conservatory staging. Plants are easily propagated from 5–8cm (2–3in) tip cuttings, taken during spring or early summer. It is best to renew plants frequently, as young plants are more attractive than older specimens.

Pennisetum alopecuroides
(P. compressum)

Grown for its handsome flowers and arching foliage, this moderately hardy herbaceous perennial, commonly known as Chinese fountain grass, has a tufted habit of growth, producing a fountain of narrow medium-green leaves, about 45cm (1½ft) in length. Towards the end of summer and into autumn, the plant sports bristly cylindrical spikes of yellowish flowers, up to 20cm (8in) in length, which are excellent for drying. So distinctive is the overall habit of this grass that it is recommended for specimen planting. It should, however, be provided with a sheltered site. Plants reach a height of 90cm (3ft), with a spread of 60cm (2ft). There is also a form on offer named 'Virescens'.

Phalaris arundinacea var. picta

Gardener's garters is one of the most striking of the white-and-green-striped grasses, but unfortunately it is also one of the most rampant, spreading vigorously by means of rhizomes. It can, however, be kept in check by forking out surplus growth. Due to its spreading habit, this hardy herbaceous perennial grass makes an excellent choice for ground cover and is especially suitable for stabilizing banks. It is also recommended ´ for mixed borders, making a marvellous foil for strongly-coloured perennials, such as bright pink, red, orange or purple phloxes. It also associates beautifully with many shrubs – try it, for example, with a purple-leaved cotinus. Flowers are produced in summer, but they are not particularly attractive. Gardener's garters reaches a height, in flower, of 90cm (3ft), with an indefinite spread.

Phyllostachys aurea

Known either as golden bamboo or as fishpole bamboo, this is a moderately hardy evergreen bamboo of graceful clump-forming habit, with vivid green canes which eventually change to creamy yellow. There is a swelling below each joint or node. Leaves grow up to 15cm (6in) in length and are medium green. Plants reach a height of 6–7m (19–22ft), with an indefinite spread. This is best used as a specimen, but is also suitable for forming a screen.

Phyllostachys bambusoides

Timber bamboo is noted for its bold, wide leaves. The new canes are a dark, shiny green, but change through yellow green to brown. This bamboo is evergreen and forms large clumps, with a height of 6–7m (19–22ft) and an indefinite spread. It is ideal for creating a screen and is also good for specimen planting.

The striking *Phalaris arundinacea* var. *picta* looks good in borders

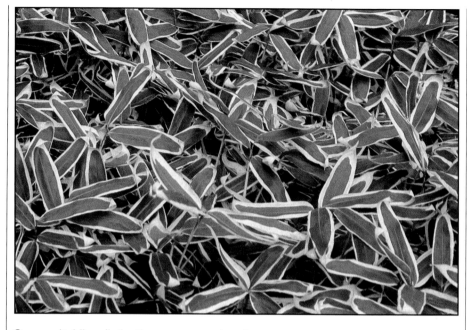

Sasa veitchii, a distinctive evergreen bamboo

Phyllostachys nigra 'Boryana'

Black bamboo is a very handsome evergreen bamboo, noted for its profusion of luxuriantly leafy and arching canes, which start off green but then change to yellow with purple splashes. The plant reaches a height of up to 4m (14ft), with an indefinite spread, and is a superb bamboo for specimen planting.

Sasa tessellata

This hardy evergreen bamboo forms dense thickets of thin vivid-green canes and has broad glossy-green leaves up to 60cm (2ft) in length. It makes excellent tall ground cover, having a height of up to 1.8m (6ft), with an indefinite spread.

Sasa veitchii

(Sasa albomarginata)

This very hardy evergreen bamboo forms lower thickets than S. *tessellata*, up to 1.2m (4ft) high, with an indefinite spread, and is also recommended for ground cover. The canes start purple-green, but later change to purple. The wide leaves grow up to 25cm (10in) in length, the margins dying back in autumn and becoming hay coloured – an attractive feature.

Sesleria heufleriana

Balkan blue grass is an unusual but attractive evergreen perennial grass, grown for its foliage. Of tufted habit, it has dark-green leaves with grey-green undersides. Purple flowers are produced in the spring. This very hardy grass has a height of 45cm (1½ft) and a spread of 30–45cm (1–1½ft). It is useful for edging a border or gravel area.

Setaria glauca

(Setaria lutescens)

Yellow bristle grass is a half-hardy annual grass noted for its decorative

44

flower heads, which are produced in summer. The reddish-gold, spike-like heads are 12.5cm (5in) long and are bristly and suitable for drying. The plant has a height of 45cm (1½ft), with a spread of 10–15cm (4–6in). Sow seeds outdoors, when the risk of frost is over, in a warm sunny sheltered border.

Shibataea kumasasa

This low-growing, very hardy evergreen bamboo forms clumps that make pleasing ground cover. It is very leafy, with broad green leaves about 10cm (4in) in length. The branching zigzag canes are a green brown. This bamboo has a height of 1–1.5m (3–5ft), with a spread of 30cm (1ft), and is particularly recommended for moist soil.

Spartina pectinata 'Aureo Marginata'

(*S.p.* 'Aureo-variegata')
This is a tall herbaceous perennial grass with long arching leaves. They are striped with yellow and green, becoming an attractive warm brown shade in autumn and winter. Plumes of purple and green flowers are produced in summer. This grass has a height of 1.8m (6ft), with an indefinite spread, extended by means of rhizomes. It is a useful and distinctive grass for inclusion in mixed borders or gravel areas, but avoid planting it in very dry soils.

ABOVE *Spartina pectinata* 'Aureo Marginata'
BELOW *Sesleria heufleriana*

Stenotaphrum secundatum
'Variegatum'

Stenotaphrum secundatum 'Variegatum'

Variegated St Augustine or buffalo grass is a tender evergreen perennial grass, grown as a houseplant or conservatory plant. It needs a minimum temperature of 13°C (56°F). About 15cm (6in) high, it spreads indefinitely by means of creeping stems that root at the nodes or joints. Its striking, blunt-ended leaves are striped with green and cream. Brown-green spike-like flowers are produced in summer, but are not particularly attractive. Buffalo grass is ideal for hanging baskets or other elevated containers, where it is best grown in soil-based potting compost. Propagate frequently from cuttings consisting of a tuft of leaves on a short length of stem, as young plants are best.

Stipa arundinacea

Pheasant grass is an unusual and moderately hardy perennial grass from New Zealand, grown for its foliage. Of tufted habit, it produces 30cm (1ft) long brown-green leaves, which become orange towards the end of summer. During the autumn attractive pendulous sprays of purple-green flowers are produced. Its height when in flower is 1.5m (5ft), with a spread of 1.2m (4ft). It is suitable for a mixed border, and will tolerate a minimum temperature of −5°C (23°F).

Stipa calamagrostis
(Achnatherum calamagrostis)

A very hardy evergreen perennial grass, forming dense tufts, this has leaves that roll inwards, making them rush-like, and that are blue-green in colour. This grass is noted

Stipa arundinacea

for its attractive buff-coloured feathery plumes of flowers, which are produced in summer and are suitable for drying. It can reach a height of up to 1.2m (4ft), with a spread of 60cm (2ft). This evergreen can be used to good advantage as an isolated specimen – in a lawn, say – and is also effective in a gravel area, where you might like to contrast it with broader-leaved plants.

Stipa gigantea

Golden oats is a large, densely-tufted perennial grass, which makes a superb specimen in a lawn or

46

Stipa pennata

Zea mays 'Gracillima Variegata'

gravel area. The evergreen rush-like leaves, which are a grey-green colour, grow to at least 45cm (1½ft) in length, and during summer large sprays of yellowish flowers are produced. These remain attractive well into winter. Golden oats is moderately hardy with a height of 2.4m (8ft), and a spread of 90cm (3ft).

Stipa pennata
A hardy perennial, feather grass is densely tufted with medium-green leaves that are very narrow. During summer it produces impressive feathery plumes of silver-buff flowers; these are suitable for drying for winter decoration. Plants are up to 90cm (3ft) high, with a spread of 45cm (1½ft). Feather grass makes a handsome specimen plant, and is also suitable for gravel areas.

Stipa tenacissima
Esparto grass is a perennial that is moderately hardy and very densely tufted. Its leaves are bright green, narrow and rush-like, and in summer there are attractive feathery flower heads. The plant has a height of 60–90cm (2–3ft), with a similar spread. This is a fine specimen or border plant, and it will also make a fine show in a gravel area.

Zea mays
Ornamental maize, or sweet corn, is a half-hardy annual that is generally used as a dot plant in summer bedding schemes, where it provides height and contrast. It is an ideal choice for a sub-tropical bedding scheme, but is also useful for mixed borders. Grow it in a position that is sheltered from strong winds. Sweet corn forms a tall thick stem, bearing long, broad, lance-shaped leaves. Silky flowers are produced in summer, followed by erect cobs containing the seeds. Ornamental cultivars include 'Gigantea Quadricolor': this has light yellow, white and pink variegated leaves and yellow cobs, the plant reaching a height of 1–2m (3–6ft), with a spread of 60cm (2ft). Another striking cultivar, 'Gracillima Variegata', has leaves boldly striped with cream and green, and bright yellow cobs. This plant reaches a height of 90cm (3ft), with a spread of 30–45cm (1–1½ft). Seeds should be raised under glass in midspring. Sow them individually in small pots and germinate at 18°C (65°F). After hardening young plants in a garden frame, plant them outdoors, when the danger of frost is over. Seeds may also be sown outdoors *in situ* during late spring.

INDEX AND ACKNOWLEDGEMENTS

Page numbers in **bold type** indicate illustrations

Picture credits
Gillian Beckett: 25(t), 38, 40(b), 43(b).
Derek Gould: 7, 29(tl), 36(tr), 42, 43(tr).
Peter McHoy: 14.
S. & O. Mathews: 35.
Harry Smith Horticultural Collection: 1, 4-5, 6, 8, 9, 10, 11(tl),
    12, 13, 15(cr,b), 17(tr,bl), 18, 19, 21, 22, 24, 28, 30(tr), 31, 32, 36(b),
    37, 39(c,b), 47(tl).
Michael Warren: 11(tr), 16, 25(b), 26-27, 29(tr), 30(bl), 33(bl,br),
    34(t,b), 40(t), 41, 46(tl,cr), 47(tr).

Artwork by Simon Roulstone